P9-DWE-906

DESERTED
PRISONS

by Joyce Markovics

Consultant: Ursula Bielski
Author and Paranormal Researcher
Founder of Chicago Hauntings, Inc.

BEARPORT
PUBLISHING

New York, New York

Credits

Cover, © Zorandim/Shutterstock and © nienora/Shutterstock; TOC, © City of Angels/Shutterstock; 4–5, © Nagel Photography/Shutterstock and © iJeab/Shutterstock; 6, © Everett Collection Historical/Alamy; 7, © Alistar James/Alamy; 8, © Private Collection/Courtesy of Swann Auction Galleries/Bridgeman Images; 9, © karenfoleyphotography/Shutterstock; 10, © James Chandler/Dreamstime; 11, © Nagel Photography/Shutterstock; 12, © Chalabala/iStock; 13, © beer5020/iStock; 14, Public Domain; 15, © Tim Kiser/CC BY-SA 2.5; 16T, Public Domain; 16B, © Tim Kiser/CC BY-SA 2.5; 17, © bonciutoma/iStock; 18, © Maciej Bledowski/Shutterstock; 19, © Plus69/Shutterstock; 20, © GlebStock/Shutterstock; 21, © Todd Bannor/Alamy; 23, © Asmus Koefoed/Shutterstock and © photocritical/Shutterstock; 24, © Chaowalit Seeneha/Shutterstock.

Publisher: Kenn Goin
Senior Editor: Joyce Tavolacci
Creative Director: Spencer Brinker
Photo Researcher: Thomas Persano
Cover: Kim Jones

Library of Congress Cataloging-in-Publication Data

Names: Markovics, Joyce L., author.
Title: Deserted prisons / by Joyce Markovics.
Description: New York : Bearport Publishing Company, Inc., 2017. | Series:
    Tiptoe into scary places | Includes bibliographical references and index.
Identifiers: LCCN 2016042368 (print) | LCCN 2016046454 (ebook) | ISBN
    9781684020522 (library) | ISBN 9781684021048 (ebook)
Subjects: LCSH: Haunted prisons—Juvenile literature. | Haunted
    prisons—United States—Juvenile literature.
Classification: LCC BF1477.3 .M37 2017 (print) | LCC BF1477.3 (ebook) | DDC
    133.1/22—dc23
LC record available at https://lccn.loc.gov/2016042368

For more information, write to Bearport Publishing Company, Inc., 45 West 21st Street, Suite 3B, New York, New York 10010. Printed in the United States of America.

10 9 8 7 6 5 4 3 2 1

CONTENTS

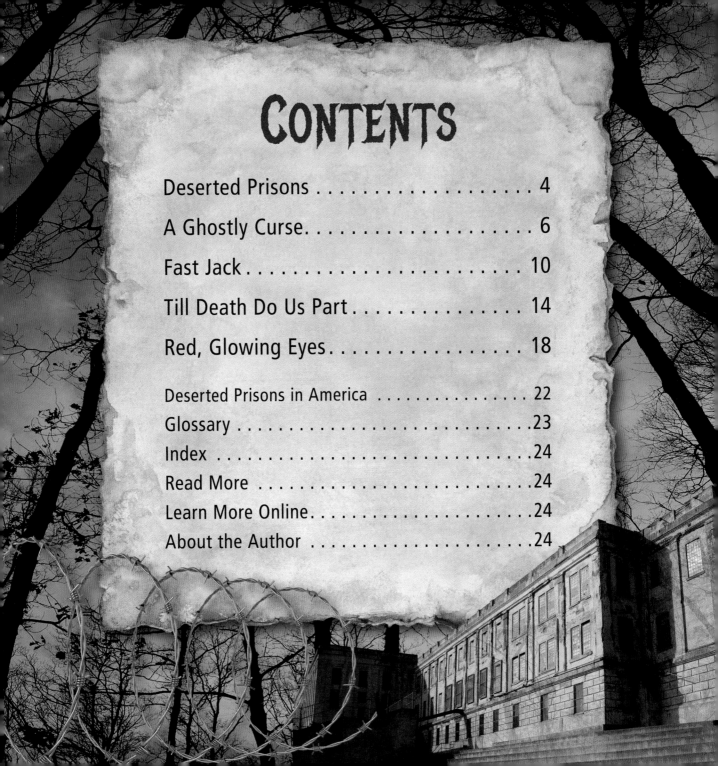

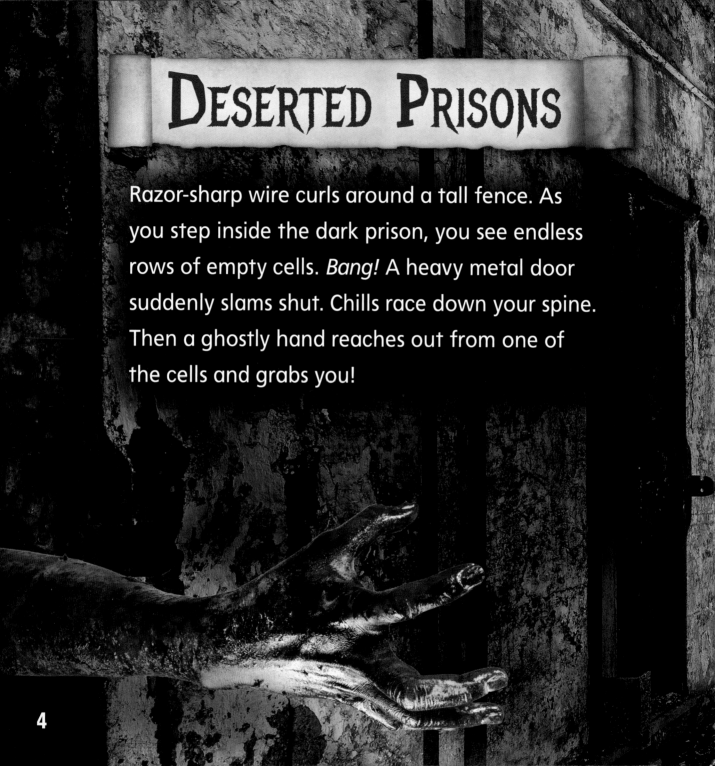

DESERTED PRISONS

Razor-sharp wire curls around a tall fence. As you step inside the dark prison, you see endless rows of empty cells. *Bang!* A heavy metal door suddenly slams shut. Chills race down your spine. Then a ghostly hand reaches out from one of the cells and grabs you!

Get ready to read four frightening tales about deserted prisons. Turn the page . . . if you have the nerve!

5

A GHOSTLY CURSE

Eastern State Penitentiary, Philadelphia, Pennsylvania
Opened 1829 • Closed 1971

From the outside, the prison looks like a castle. However, its thick walls hold many dark secrets.

Over the years, about 80,000 **criminals** were locked up in the prison. One of the most famous was Al Capone, a Chicago gangster. Yet even Al wasn't tough enough to fight off a ghost.

Al Capone

Eastern State
Penitentiary

7

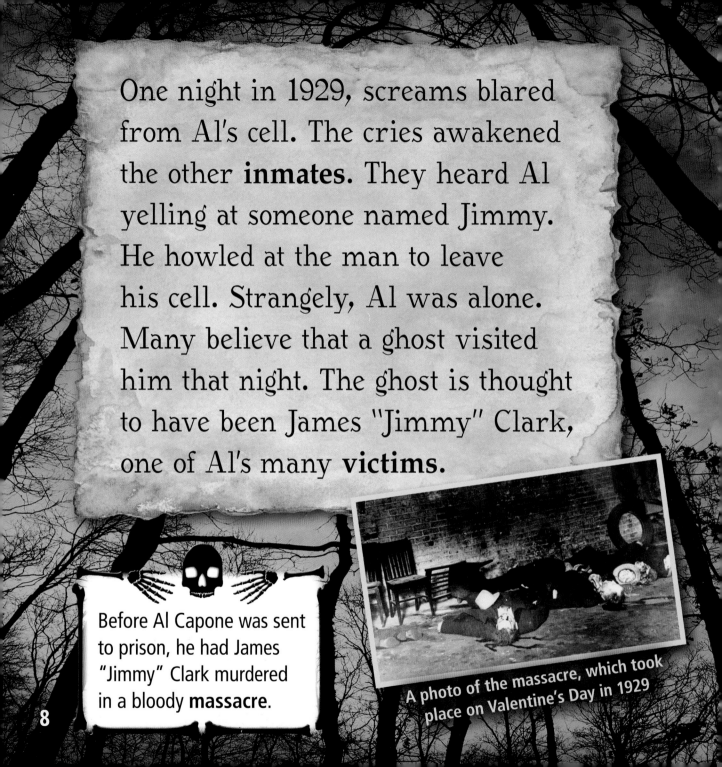

One night in 1929, screams blared from Al's cell. The cries awakened the other **inmates**. They heard Al yelling at someone named Jimmy. He howled at the man to leave his cell. Strangely, Al was alone. Many believe that a ghost visited him that night. The ghost is thought to have been James "Jimmy" Clark, one of Al's many **victims**.

Before Al Capone was sent to prison, he had James "Jimmy" Clark murdered in a bloody **massacre**.

A photo of the massacre, which took place on Valentine's Day in 1929

Al Capone's cell

9

FAST JACK

Missouri State Penitentiary, Jefferson City, Missouri
Opened 1836 • Closed 2004

There's a prison in Missouri with a long and bloody past. It was once the largest prison in the country. After it closed, the prison became home to a **mischievous** spirit named Fast Jack.

Missouri State Penitentiary

Fast Jack is believed to be the ghost of a former prisoner. **Witnesses** have spotted him racing down hallways. Some have even seen him pop out of the walls. Then, *poof!* He's gone.

When he was alive, Fast Jack is thought to have run **errands** in the prison.

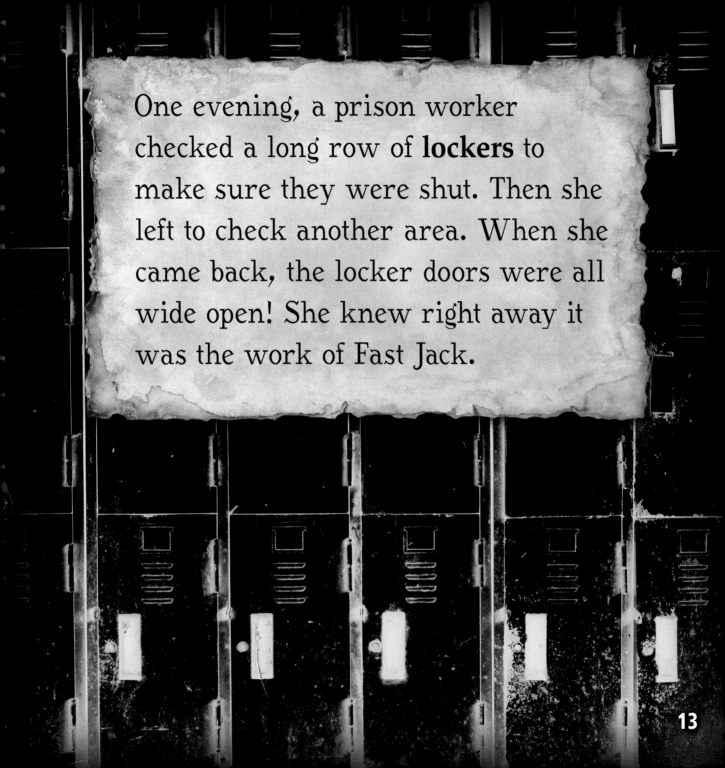

One evening, a prison worker checked a long row of **lockers** to make sure they were shut. Then she left to check another area. When she came back, the locker doors were all wide open! She knew right away it was the work of Fast Jack.

Till Death Do Us Part

West Virginia State Penitentiary, Moundsville, West Virginia
Opened 1876 • Closed 1995

Would you believe that a ghost could send a man to prison? In West Virginia in 1897, that's what many believe happened.

One day, Zona Heaster Shue was found dead. The young bride's body lay in a heap at the bottom of a staircase. Soon after, her shocked husband, Trout Shue, buried her body. Her death was ruled an accident. But was it really?

Zona Heaster Shue

West Virginia
State Penitentiary

15

A month after the death, Zona's mother was visited by her daughter's ghost. The spirit told her that she had been murdered by Trout. Soon after, Zona's body was dug up. A doctor discovered that she had been choked to death! Trout was found **guilty** of murder. He spent the rest of his life in the state prison in Moundsville.

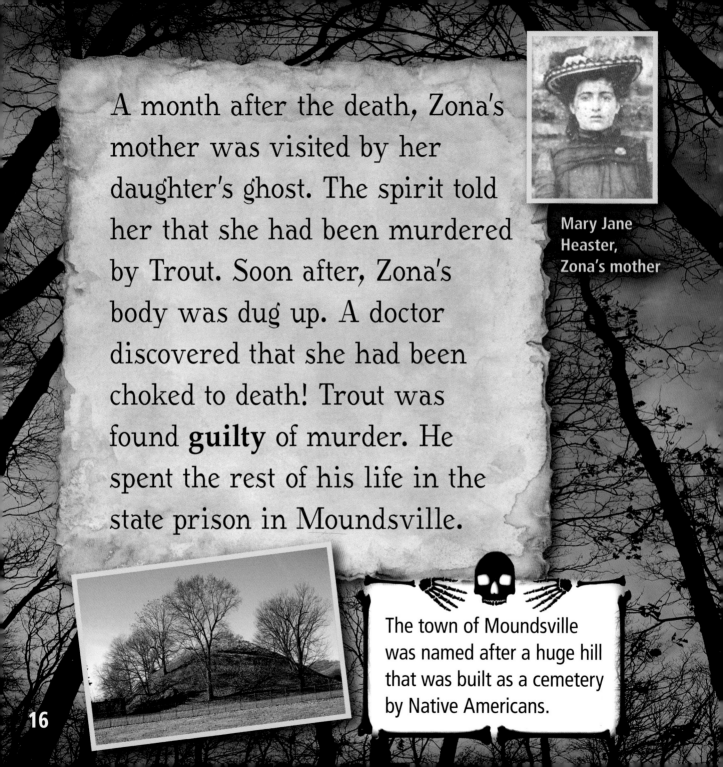

Mary Jane Heaster, Zona's mother

The town of Moundsville was named after a huge hill that was built as a cemetery by Native Americans.

RED, GLOWING EYES

Alcatraz Federal Penitentiary, San Francisco, California
Opened 1934 • Closed 1963

Alcatraz sits on a tiny, rocky island. When the prison was in use, it was a harsh and lonely place. It's no surprise that some of its inmates met a terrible **fate** there.

In the 1940s, an inmate was thrown into a dark, tiny cell called "the hole" for bad behavior. Within seconds of being locked in, the man cried out for help. He told the guards that a creature with red, glowing eyes was in the cell with him. The guards ignored his cries.

Over the years, more than 35 prisoners have tried to escape from Alcatraz. None succeeded and many drowned in the process.

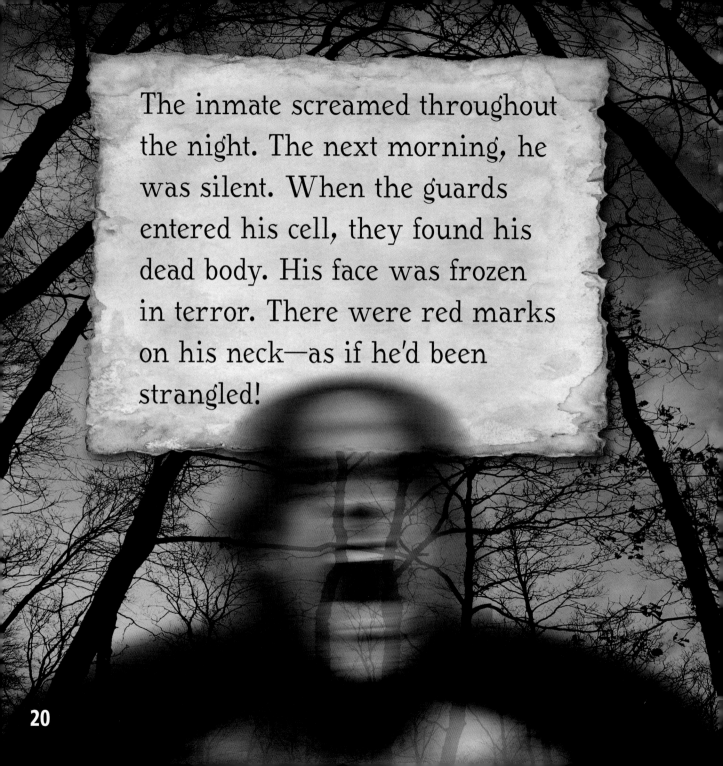

The inmate screamed throughout the night. The next morning, he was silent. When the guards entered his cell, they found his dead body. His face was frozen in terror. There were red marks on his neck—as if he'd been strangled!

"The hole" at Alcatraz

DESERTED PRISONS
IN AMERICA

ALCATRAZ FEDERAL PENITENTIARY

San Francisco, California

Explore one of the world's harshest and scariest prisons.

MISSOURI STATE PENITENTIARY

Jefferson City, Missouri

Visit a place where a mischief-making spirit still roams.

EASTERN STATE PENITENTIARY

Philadelphia, Pennsylvania

Learn about an old prison once filled with criminals . . . and their victims' ghosts!

WEST VIRGINIA STATE PENITENTIARY

Moundsville, West Virginia

Check out a prison that was home to a murdering mastermind.

NORTH AMERICA

EUROPE

ASIA

Atlantic Ocean

Pacific Ocean

AFRICA

Pacific Ocean

SOUTH AMERICA

Indian Ocean

Atlantic Ocean

AUSTRALIA

Southern Ocean

ANTARCTICA

N
W   E
S

GLOSSARY

criminals (KRIM-uh-nuhlz) people who have broken the law

errands (ERR-uhnds) quick trips made to accomplish something, such as delivering a package

fate (FAYT) the force that some people believe controls events and decides the future

guilty (GIL-tee) having done something wrong or against the law

inmates (IN-mayts) prisoners

lockers (LAHK-*urz*) compartments or drawers that may be locked and are used for storage

massacre (MASS-uh-kur) the brutal killing of a large number of people

mischievous (MISS-chuh-vuhs) playfully annoying

victims (VIK-tuhmz) people who have been hurt or killed

witnesses (WIT-niss-ez) people who tell what they saw

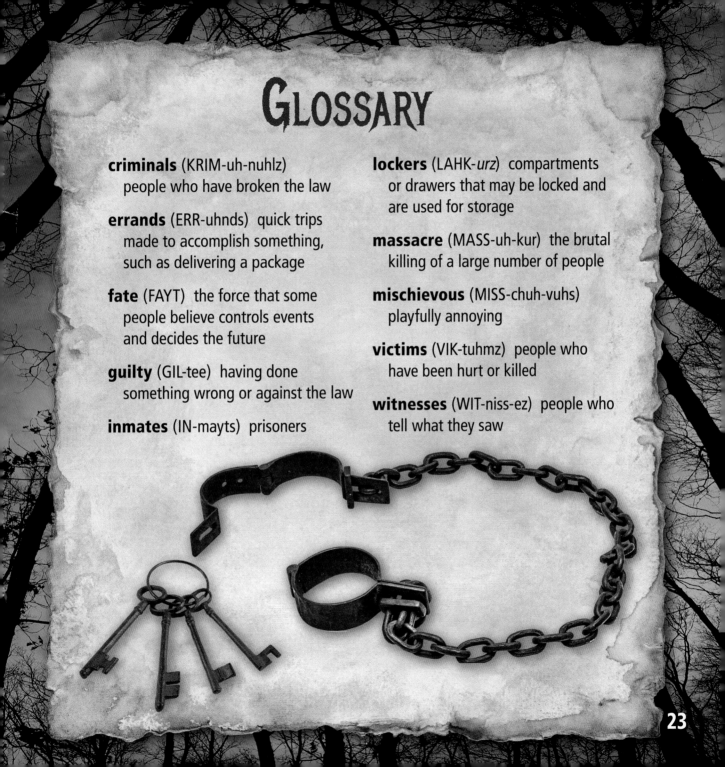

Index

Read More

Penn-Coughin, O. *They're Coming For You: Scary Stories that Scream to be Read.* Bend, OR: You Come Too (2011).

Phillips, Dee. *Doomed on Death Row (Cold Whispers II).* New York: Bearport (2017).

Learn More Online

To learn more about deserted prisons, visit:
www.bearportpublishing.com/Tiptoe

About the Author

Joyce Markovics lives in a
160-year-old house. Chances are a few
otherworldly beings live there, too.